The Headless Angel

Praise for *The Headless Angel*

Sometimes I feel there is nothing more holy than encountering a Bill Brown poem. For this poet, church is found "Sunday on the Ridge" with the metronome of a cat's tail and the hymnal of tree leaves. Brown softly enters the lush pastoral landscapes of his past and present life, weaving personal slices of memory and myth with the vibrant theater of nature like "a crocus blossom in the snow" or "A sea of broom sage...." These incredible poems are replete with cats, trees, quiet mornings with coffee, squirrels on the roof, a letter to Neruda, the lover's easy breath, and the wafting scent of fresh baked bread. Brown needles the solitude and *ongoingness* of creation with such deft mastery of language, prosody, and syntax. Each poem is a prayer, a whispered utterance of delight and glory, reaching in the dirt for the divine. This is a poet deeply connected to the earth—the forest loam—putting his ear to the sacred ground by translating the abstract feelings of loss and hope and grief and family. The older poet is still the young boy rubbing birch bark in the dark. The older poet is still my first mentor, the one who taught me the wonderment of words. This book is a testament to his incredible life and love for the "deepening with questions" and the "Heart in throat words" swirling all around and through the sanctuaries inside us. "How paying attention makes the world specific / and the names that name it": this is ultimately what Bill Brown taught me and keeps teaching me through his voluminous work: precision and connection—the human tapestry weaving your life to mine, to the readers and back again. This book is a constant communion.

—Tiana Clark

In "What Light There Is," Bill Brown writes: "...inside the heart's / closet where there / are no empty hangers, / dreams bargain..." The poems in this collection are rich with such wisdom and beauty, each bargaining for a second, a third read, and more. Brown's words resonate with what's deepest in our hearts. If I'm ever sent to that desert island where we can take only a handful of books, *The Headless Angel* will have to be among them.

—Cathy Ann Kodra

The Headless Angel

Poems

Bill Brown

Iris Press
Oak Ridge, Tennessee

Copyright © 2020 by Bill Brown

All rights reserved. No portion of this book may be reproduced in any form or by any means, including electronic storage and retrieval systems, without explicit, prior written permission of the publisher, except for brief passages excerpted for review and critical purposes.

Cover and Book Design by Robert B. Cumming, Jr.

Library of Congress Cataloging-in-Publication Data

Names: Brown, Bill, 1948 September 17- author.
Title: The headless angel : poems / Bill Brown.
Description: Oak Ridge, Tennessee : Iris Press, [2020] | Summary: "The Headless Angel is a poetry collection divided into two sections, "The Truest Myth," and "What the Soul Ate." Bill Brown wrote these poems in his mid-sixties to explore aging, and surviving in this "often dark world" by paying attention to moments, solitude and the Creative Spirit of our natural world. Living in the Milky Way with over 300 billion stars, an un-understandable figure, is a true gift beyond our knowing. The poems are grouped seasonally, many are love poems to life, his wife, Suzanne, and the precious struggle to live each day at a time. Other poems reach back into his life's journey with new visions. Come, take this journey with him"— Provided by publisher.
Identifiers: LCCN 2020004933 | ISBN 9781604542639 (paperback)
Subjects: LCGFT: Poetry.
Classification: LCC PS3552.R68523 H43 2020 | DDC 811/.54—dc23
LC record available at https://lccn.loc.gov/2020004933

Acknowledgments

Thanks to the editors of the following journals and anthologies in which these poems first appeared.

Allegro: "Infant Sun"
Atlanta Review: "My Mother," "Taps"
Aurorean: "The Truest Myth" (Pushcart Nominee), "What Light There Is"
Big Muddy: "Church of Childhood," "Morning Instructions," "Sage"
Birmingham Arts Journal: "Startle"
Broad River Review: "Evening Song"
Cleaver: "November's Edge," "Openings"
Cloudbank: "Falling," "Late Autumn Fugue"
Clover: "Of," "Saturday on the Ridge"
Columbia Journal: "Drive," "Post Contemporary Lorca," "Sleep," "The Muse"
Conclave: "Arabella," "Sunrise at the Cemetery"
Cumberland River Review: "Certain Words," "Dawn Tugs"
Evening Street Review: "Doze," "Stardust"
Free State Review: "Today's News"
Louisville Review: "Night Creek with Goats," "Redecorate"
Nashville Anthology: "A Deepening"
Nashville Magazine: "Alters"
Number One: "County Braille," "Last Visit," "On a Cloudy August Day," "Ness," "Parting Letter," "Thanksgiving, 1962," "Wonder"
Oyster River Pages: "The Headless Angel"
POEM: "Beside Me," "Gathering Windfalls," "Goodnight Shadows," "Hilltop Musings," "Sulphur Fork," "Waiting, September Morning"
Potomac Review: "St. Simons I," "Verbs"
Poetry South: "Always," "Knock, Knock"
Southern Poetry Review: "Some Days," "Upon Waking," "Writing Lesson"
Still: the Journal: "Hollow Step," "What Lasts"
Tar River Poetry: "House"
Visions International: "Traffic Salvation"
Worcester Review: "Drey"

Contents

Section I: The Truest Myth

On a Cloudy August Day • 11
The Truest Myth • 12
Parting Letter • 13
Waiting, September Morning • 14
Falling • 15
Today's News • 16
November's Edge • 18
Late Autumn Fugue • 19
The Muse • 20
Sunday on the Ridge • 21
Thanksgiving, 1962 • 22
Touch • 23
Beside Me • 25
Wonder • 27
Openings • 29
Sage • 30
Drey • 31
A Startle • 32
Of: • 34
What Light There Is • 36
Altars • 37
The Headless Angel • 38
Drive • 39
Sulfur Fork • 40
Gathering Windfalls • 41
Dawn Tugs • 43
Taps • 45
The Scent of Fresh Baked Bread • 46
Doze • 47
Knock, Knock • 48
A Deepening • 50
Certain Words • 51
Post Contemporary Lorca • 52
Always • 53
Upon Waking • 54

St. Simons Morning I • 55
Evening Song • 56

Section II: What the Soul Ate

What Lasts • 59
Stardust • 61
Last Visit • 62
The Hollow Step • 63
Arabella • 64
Church of Childhood • 66
Infant Sun • 68
County Braille • 69
Hilltop Musings • 71
Traffic Salvation • 72
Morning Instructions • 74
Night Creek with Goats • 75
Some Days • 76
Sleep • 77
Sunrise at the Cemetery • 78
Seeing • 80
Verbs • 81
My Mother • 82
House • 84
Ness • 86
Redecorate • 88
Goodnight Shadows • 90

I

The Truest Myth

On a Cloudy August Day

The sun settles for less,
warms the tops of clouds,

converts shadows to mild shade,
lets river reflect gray, lets

current mind gravity's purpose
without glimmer, doesn't

shimmer eddies behind
the big rock where children

wade to sit and watch swallows
dance for gnats. Like sun,

river understands time,
has faith that I don't know,

except at 65, my shoulders
hunker the sky's weight,

the pulling and pushing
dark matter must offer

the Milky Way. I accept
whatever wants me closer

to earth as a kind of prayer
spoken to worms and finches,

mold and fungus, oak and maple.
On this gray day I teach myself

to care. I kneel, put my ear
to the ground, listen.

The Truest Myth

My mother
once told me
the cord behind
my navel
is still connected
to forest loam,

to sea depths,
to hilltop ponds
found north to south
by migrating birds,
to the first willow
green of late March,

to the last maple leaf
October refuses to release,
until a storm is
ordered to complete
the cycle so the sun
and its minions won't

stop myriad motions
of the darkest dust,
so the apple that hit
Newton's head won't
rise back and connect,
erasing all of our past,

sending us east
of Eden to wander
the land of Nod,
blanking our joys
and the sorrows that
made us love them.

Parting Letter

Now that the bones are gone who lives in the final dust?
—Pablo Neruda

Dear Pablo,

The final dust will blow
   my bones off Black Balsam Bald,

will give them back to honeysuckle
   and wake robin, to morning glory

and clover. Bees will carry them
   on their feet with pollen,

will buzz them with their wings.
   And when cloud fog takes

the hemlock and junipers,
   particles of my dust

will rejoice in what
   might have been sorrow,

might have been grace,
   but now coats grape vines,

     a tangle of lace.

Waiting, September Morning

September morning,
second day of clouds,
fifties late summer chill,
setting a stage, mother says
from memory's grave,
as if October, a play.
Ibsen, perhaps—who's knocking?
Or Chekov, who *is* this character?

On the porch there's a breeze
that makes a chorus of leaves,
black gum, maple, oak—as if
to welcome, but no one's coming
but me, center stage with coffee
and the cat begging for cheese—
I've rehearsed well, no need for words.

For some unknowable reason
I'm reminded of a movie
in San Francisco, 1968:
a faucet dripping while
the national anthem plays.
We watched kids on acid
pretend a plot: my commune
hippie days when we would
save the world.

Now, at 66,
I make a cool September morning
a blessing, goldfinches at feeder
enter stage right, yellow feathers
tinged winter hazel. Godot
hasn't come, but I don't mind
waiting. Me and the cat,
coffee and cheese.

Falling

> *The sunlight continues its dying fall.*
> —Charles Wright

What isn't falling,　　earth's gravity,　　sky's weight,

shrinking us　　as　　we age,

energy and matter　　so close,　　so close

until　　it is one.　　Isn't something

grand about our　　decay,　　our ashes

remaining to be　　part of something new,　　something old.

And if there is　　an eternity,　　we will be

part of　　"to be"　　forever…

each of us　　an inheritance,　　from millions

of years　　of others.　　Fall,

an October word, as leaves　　drift in breeze

past my window　　to rejoin　　rejoin,

and heaven　　is one　　of countless words

we have made　　can use　　and dream

　　　　　　　　　　　　　　　without.

Today's news

got lost when
   a sharp-shinned hawk

scooped up a chipmunk
   in front of my car—

its talons out,
   wings spread,

striped tail
   sharply marked—

and before
   I could brake,

the prey was flown
   into forest hedge

on Old Distillery Road.
   Breathless, I pulled

off the side bank
   of Sulfur Fork,

breathed deep
   before continuing

down that narrow,
   curvy trip—saying

thankyou, breeze entering
   cracked window, thankyou

hearts-a-busting blooming,
  thanks pileated woodpecker

trailing territorial laughter
  through sycamores.

November's Edge

Wake to a quiet rain touching the windows,
streaming down the slant porch roof
into the Rose of Sharon, a thousand blossoms
long gone at November's edge, another
October preparing for dismissal.
Out the study window, yellow-brown
hickory, red-green gum, and maples
with their degrees of orange-crimson—
how kind for trees to dress before winter's
vault is eased shut and locked, how sad
the word *yearning* is introduced to describe
the inexplicable. Something akin to shyness
accompanies the heart, a hungry child,
too polite to ask, watches the last piece
of cake served to her brother.

Late Autumn Fugue

Today an unwinding exists in clouds,
a slow separation as a ribbon of starlings
    imitates heaven's fugue, interweaving
as they fly, a composition with a silent
    theme, a late November theme, joined
by wind in brown oak leaves, joined
    by a temple pulse that says you're alive.
The fates are on vacation: incarnations
    of destiny use their white robes as
beach towels and watch the sun drift
    westward over the ocean. Give particle
physics a rest. Let crows call the shots today.
    Picture a woman at a window: brown eyes
reflect, remind her of the girl she was, how
    a season's change presents a longing
for a past, a future. She thinks of a boy
    who didn't make it home from war; he
will always remain a boy in memory,
    barely a shadow of a beard when he left,
how his lips thinned when he smiled.
    She takes down a book of poems
from a shelf, a page turned down
    to Emily, *because I could not stop*
for death, she whispers. Today is
    Black Friday. She will walk through
the woods to Shaker Creek and listen
    to current ripple before winter
ice-rings stones. Her thoughts will join
    the unwinding clouds, sky's
starling ribbon, interweaving as they fly.

The Muse

Today the muse sits
on the porch with the cat,
watches her nap,
peers into feline dreams—
chipmunk, mouse, sparrow.

The muse looks up,
admires how a maple leaf
sails the yard, stamps
a red print in the moss.

She leaves the cat
to its hunger, wanders
pasture edge, considers
romp and play of two
colts, bay and paint.

She understands
the crow's comment
on how milkweed
bejewels the sunny air.

As she gathers moments,
the day composes
an argument
with the cemetery.

The dead join in
about time and its
thoughtless promises—
a child's grave graced
with a marble angel
holds a cup
of last night's rain.

Sunday on the Ridge

The editor of a new book says no pet poems.
    But as I write, Mr. Dodo, the black cat,

sleeps beside my computer or peeks out the window
    as waxwings harvest a gnat hatch in hedge tangle.

His tail metronomes, clueing me to rhythm, which
    doesn't always work. The conversational tone

of Sunday on a Tennessee ridge tends
    more rustic than hymnal. Tractors instead

of church pews. Call and response—
    towhee and coyote or the neighbor's mongrels

chasing squirrels. Yet, light is always holy
    in November as black gum and maple leaves

twirl to ground and broken clouds teach
    the pond surface new shapes.

I almost expect a stranger named Jesus to walk
    across the water, pick up the puzzle pieces

and start over again, as if human hearts might
    change in late fall, as if the sky held

answers, and we might get it right this time
    before the solstice, its shortened days,

and the pit in the stomach darkens, and breathing
    finally becomes a prayer.

Thanksgiving, 1962

Father carved the turkey in the kitchen,
sat at the head of the table as Mother
brought the loaded tray. Brother's
erratic expression disapproved of green beans.

When Grandmother announced *people were
starving in China,* he offered to mail his overnight.
Sister sat picking egg out of the gravy
before the blessing, as we bowed our heads.

Our lips mouthed his prayer: *Bless this food
to the nourishment of our bodies and our
bodies to thy service. Amen.* My attention
clung to the clink of ice tea on crystal,

the scrape of forks against china
we ate on twice a year. My brother's
green beans and napkin disappeared,
a wet bulge in his pocket. Soon he would

excuse himself, and the old plumbing
announced a toilet flush upstairs.
Father thought of a nap in his chair
by the fire. Grandmother remembered

her last dinner with Papa. Sister
wondered if the heroine in her novel
would find her way, brother was ready
for a pickup game in the Rogers' yard.

Mother questioned why there were
always green beans in the pickle relish.
The spaniel and sparrows on the back porch
dreamed of leftovers, truly thankful.

Touch

The sun whispers dawn
in November's yellow leaves
so as not to wake me.

I read that frogs sang their songs
before the human strand became
warm-blooded.

Are eulogies tributes to death as well
as those who die—can words hold
grief as tightly as human hands?

Empty fingers carry a heavy load—
reach to hold something—
always my wife's shoulders.

Touch means physical contact,
to rouse tender or painful feelings,
to steal.

Touch-me-not is a flower
that explodes seeds
when touched.

When you *lose touch*, you cease
talking. *Touch and go* is risky.
Keep in touch.

The sunset eases into the pond
just as it eases around the planet—
pink then mauve then blue.

Tree frogs trill their ancient song
in spring, climb deep in wood crevices
to winter.

Evening whispers in the same leaves as
dawn, and night's a polished stone,
smooth to touch.

Beside Me

They come at night:
   quiet house,
      cats asleep
         on the stairs,

light from a distant
   farmhouse,
      a shuddered glint.
         Your easy breath
            beside me.

They come: the years,
   our upstairs apartment
      on Belmont,
         our first cottage
            beside an orchard

and now this home
   we've lived in longer,
      your breath,
         your tangled hair.

Just yesterday I woke,
   slipped down stairs,
      turned on coffee,
         fed cats.

Zero degrees on the porch,
   mockingbird and towhee
      eating suet together,
         a winter truce.

    I said your name
      in a whisper,
        so as not to wake,
          but voice the consonants
         and vowels—

witness its sounds—
   icicles from the roof
    glistened.

Wonder

This morning, wonder swims
the sky like crows jostling
each other in flight,

or a child's breath clouding
a window,

a puppy licking leftover milk
from a cereal bowl,

a curmudgeon's lip filled
with snuff, her daydream—
a girl holding her father's
calloused hand,

maybe a pickup on gravel
road with a beagle hound
licking air out the passenger
window,

or a girl trying on her sister's
lipstick in the bathroom mirror,

or a boy running a touchdown
in the front yard, alone,

two bearded goats standing
on a shed,

a sea turtle living its
one hundred and fiftieth
year,

a white oak cathedral
filled with starlings,

your dreaming hand
reaching out for something
I can't see.

Openings

> *Blessed is the sick day.*
> *Blessed are things that open/for no reason.*
> —Lorraine Doran

Let's say a brother's left hand
opens and closes on his coffee cup.
A lover's face opens when someone
enters a room. The blessed day, being sick,
needs such nurturing, such openings—
a crocus blossom in the snow,
a door of an abandoned house,
a coffin without a corpse.
All open—
not like a switchblade,
fast and deliberate,
but like a heart valve,
its blood nutrient rich—
so the frozen crocus will re-blossom,
the abandoned house welcome
stray cats and phoebes,
and the coffin, as always,
awaits to be filled.
The blessed day awaits—
a birdfeeder surprised
by a chickadee that grubs
the last seed. I arise early,
not sad, but aware that
a lover's face will one day
exist in a framed square
above some mantel, and
memory will circle like
smoke from a chimney
in a snowy sky.

Sage

A sea of broom sage
   waves winter Tennessee hills,

protects country cemeteries
   and churches. Allied to ponds

and broken down barns,
   it befriends tattered

barbwire wrapped
   in honeysuckle vines.

Is it just me, the only
   car on this gravel road

that watches an overalled
   old man wade the field,

palming seed heads as if
   he were blessing children,

as if his hands held grace.
   Maybe today they do.

The bill of his cap neatly
   creased, his flannel sleeves

rolled up to his elbows
   so he can baptize a farmer's

ghosts in the brown
   waves of sage.

Drey

A *dray* is a low cart without sides
used for heavy loads. But until
today, I didn't know that a *drey*
was the name for a squirrel's nest.
It's the word before *dribble* in
my dictionary. I stare out
my study window and count
four dreys in oak and hickory.
Late January and gray squirrels
raid my bird feeders. They've torn
the screen on my porch, made friends
with my cats. I'd like to collect
dreys and share them with a distant
neighbor. Perhaps invite my brother
to hunt squirrels, like we did when
we were boys. I think of squirrel stew
and gag. My grandmother's law:
if you kill it, you eat it, unless it's
a rattlesnake, and that will make
a belt or hatband. Perhaps what
we learned from The Great Depression
we should remember in this *MALL* world.
So today, as the sun illuminates
leafless bones of winter trees,
I'll make peace with squirrels,
let them hang from the porch
roof and steal sunflower seed.
Let them sleep snug in their
assorted dreys. I'll be content
to learn a new word, the one
     before *dribble.*

A Startle

A startle of quail rose
   from the winter field,
      chilled my shoulders,
         as if a gust blew them

from broom sage and thicket
   to the leafless birches
      guarding Crooked Creek.
         Once I filled a bag with

birch bark to keep textured
   curls beside my bed. On
      sleepless nights, I rubbed
         them between fingers

and dreamed of water
   searching rocks.
      My father called them
         God's paper haunted

with messages.
   To me they whisper about
      morning light, another day
         to witness beauty even in

desolation—how the stark
   and lonely repeat a life-song
      in February. Beneath forest
         loam bloodroot longs

to rise above the soil.
   Joy and sorrow are
      about living,
         interpretation,

 even in
  a universe
   dancing
    in darkness.

Of:

> Expressing the relationship
> between a part and a whole

It's hard to write about snow
   without saying white, without
comparing the twine of oak limbs
   to fish bones, without praying

Scotty might beam us to a sunny
   beach in late May: Frisbees, beer
and golden retrievers, the sound
   of waves searching.

But this morning, I pause while
   sweeping a drift from the porch
and listen to a whisper of flakes
   speak at forest edge. What are they

saying—something about a gift
   of water, a trillion crystals, none
the same. Despite bird hunger and
   secret dreams of hibernating frogs,

I should pull down an old book
   and read *the world is too much*
with us late and soon... accept
   this day as a gift of solitude, a time

for making a pot of bean soup,
   a pan of cornbread, invite dead
parents for a visit—thinking that,
   I hear footsteps—sigh, because

it's squirrels on the roof. Given
　　crystals that soak loam, dark
bark of hardwoods and the little
　　abstract paintings of lichen,

fungus and algae asleep, dreaming
　　of spring, a reckoning is present,
a waiting, a becoming, the ongoing
　　of of creation.

What Light There Is

What light there is
on a rainy March morning
glows from two crocuses,
one yellow, one violet.
My mother found light
on dark days—red maple
buds whispering birth,
gloss of lady bug
on kitchen window.
She lived alone 30 years
after Father's death.
In early winter she
brought in herbs
that might die, kept
them in a spare room
to plant again in spring.
Her way to honor
Persephone. Light
is what she found,
or made, keeping
darkness at bay,
or inside the heart's
closet where there
are no empty hangers,
dreams bargain
with shadows,
and prayers call
our little sun back
for one more day.

Altars

Start with a March window,
sun ablaze to melt snow,
a birdseed scattered porch.

Cardinals, chickadees, titmice,
white-crowned sparrows,
juncos and towhees, cracking

black oil to live another day.
Necessity fills the world with altars.
Mockingbird fusses at any beaks

that near the suet. For me
red buds forming on maples
speak of roots awakening

in their earthy fungus bed,
willing to risk a hard frost
to open spring. Pretend

is human—disappointment
a selfish form of prayer. So
I'll take the shovel to the drive—

Earn your hope, father speaks
from the grave. In the road
crow has found a dead squirrel,

starts with the eyes. One's misfortune
makes another's breakfast. Today
sunshine is the door of Plato's Cave.

Winter's shadows on the wall can't
entice me to read. Crocus shoots
break sod beneath soft snow.

The Headless Angel

My wife tried to glue the head
    back on, but it's concrete and keeps

falling off. The cat tries to roll it around
    the porch floor. We bought it for

the garden to honor our dead mothers,
    but when the head fell off, we couldn't—

so it sits with the uneven chipped neck,
    kneeling with little hands folded

in prayer, wings nestled on its back.
    I thought to bury her, but can't.

My mother used to quote, *angels from
    above watch over those we love.*

This morning I put the head on a garden brick
    so it can watch tulips bloom. I place

a cap on it to shield eyes from the sun.
    I'm beginning to like this new version

of *Winged Victory,* tiny headless child.
    My wife painted its toenails bright red,

its wings, purple. Calvin said *everyone
    of us has thousands of angels attending,*

but give me this little concrete beauty,
    her head among flowers, her squat form

        always in prayer.

Drive

A certain doom follows cars on the interstate,
    speed set on 70, radio pushing products around

pop songs. Hard to notice return of redwing blackbirds
    or hear flying whispers of finches, a wobble

of turkeys grazing last year's corn stubble. Blind
    to the sun being covered by a camel-shaped cloud,

you notice McDonald's at the next exit, Taco Bell,
    Burger King. You read road signs like *Drive sober,*

or get pulled over. Or *Trucks rock, but they also roll.*
    Imagine who gets paid to write this stuff.

Turn off news about how many more troops sent to
    war, how many citizens wounded in a terrorist attack.

But car silence isn't prayerful with an eighteen-wheeler
    forcing you to slow down on a hill. You catch your

eyes in the mirror and mistake them for a person
    who once promised to honor moments, but there's

an ambulance blaring its lights and siren, each lane
    blocked, and inside you're a sparrow trapped on

the back porch, wings banging the screen, scaring
    its beak against a mesh of wire.

Sulfur Fork

Wild iris bloom beside Sulfur Fork,
tiny alligator snappers creep the pebbled shore,
and a corn snake, lovely with new skin,

s's its spring hunger toward a jeer of frogs.
Maples and sycamores have leafed enough
to offer first shade. A rotten death smell

fumes from a hopping circle of buzzards,
vying for position around a swollen doe—
death, an answer to living hunger.

The quiet of dark hollows drains winter
toward the creek, a haunting whisper
through a ceremony of ferns, a curl

above dank loam. In the forest crown
a rain crow, fresh from the Caribbean,
tock-tocks its weather report to the sky.

Gathering Windfalls

I kneel to study tiniest violets that hide
in spring grass, each a perfect miniature

of its larger cousin. Perhaps its blue shines
more vibrant. A little black buzzard

circles above, sees me crouched
in grass—I wave so it won't consider

me breakfast. Last night's storm covered
the lawn with maple buds causing

a gnat hatch, inviting a cerulean warbler
out of forest crown—the second one I've

seen in sixty-seven years. I sighted the first
canoeing the Buffalo River. Memory

knows the time and place such a color
surprises. Something prayerful rises

from earth like gnats to feed the spirit
of this March day, as I break sticks in

wheelbarrow to deposit in woodland loam.
I think of how a theologian said that

human souls hover over our heads
like cartoon bubbles and, at death,

slowly dissolve. On such a day I
almost feel my bubble expand,

like those our neighbor's child blows
into the wind, rainbow colors in

sunlight, chased by the collie,
until they rise and disappear.

Dawn Tugs

For some, dawn limps in, a gruff,
    withered nook—furtive, backdoor,
        hangdog, swigging a shot of rotgut;
            life, a wincing rut that groans
                and pulls a pillow over its head.

My father greeted dawn like a hat
    he wore into the day, beneath its rim,
        a new beginning, yesterday and tomorrow,
            gone and yet to come.

Boyhood mornings smelt of coffee
    and burnt toast, oatmeal and juice.
        A blessing said, a Bible verse, as my brother
            shot me the finger under his napkin.

Dawn tugs at the horizon,
    sculpts an orange glow
        among the moistened bark
            of March trees. First light
                rustles pine needles, seeps
                    edges of bedroom windows
                        cracked to collect a night breeze.

Today, dawn's a maple table
    patinaed with living, human habits
        scored in its surface like a map.
            Follow it with fingertips,
                a memory braille—
                    Mother's small hands,

      Father's pocket watch beside
         his cup—a day's timed labor
            from 5 a.m. to 6 p.m.
                At night, it slept on his dresser
              as he slept,

the settling
   of an old house
      waltzing to its ticks.

Taps

I find my fingers drumming the table,
kind of blue, kind of Ella, thinking
of you, of how finches and warblers
celebrate a gnat hatch, dandelion seeds,
how a light shower adds to April.

My fingers count as well, how
many taps to number those I've lost—
Mother, Father, Tommy, Ship, John…
on and on. Yet, near the back porch
Carolina wrens build a new nest.

Two mock oranges fill mornings
with white bowl-shaped blossoms.
I used to give sorrow away instead
of owning it, as if loss is not a gift,
a depth of feeling, dreaming, that

begs the importance of one's hands,
eyes, feet—how kneeling in dirt
to renew a garden, a maker's form
of prayer. Many stars that brighten
our sky might be dead, but their

energy still lights our darkness.
I remember my mother saying,
a world away and time. I'm
beginning to fathom what she felt.
This *living in the moment* important

if only you hold a life inside.
Don't live in a place where
longings are swapped for *things.*
Let loss mellow like a maple table
patinaed with use.

The Scent of Fresh Baked Bread

Mauve and gray clouds layer a western sky,
signaling an April night. Mockingbirds
and towhees share mating songs,
and American toads blur their little

pronouncements into the soft loam.
As evening stretches its arms to yawn,
porch and barn lights begin to shimmer
the ridge in an unplanned order.

Fresh bread scent drifts from loaves
cooling on a neighbor's deck.
My mother's baking day was Friday—
kids on St. John Ave. gathered behind

our house to fight over the loaf she
buttered to savor before supper.
How a scent carries me a world away,
softens my old-man's shoulders, garden sore.

The decay of years, like forest loam,
breaks down memory, leaves and wood,
creates a rich fiction of a life, perhaps
covered with soft moss and lichen,

childhood faces, first loves, deaths—
prepares the soul for mystery,
a darkness beyond one's
conscious scope. Tonight—

a moon,
    then clouds,
        a soft rain
            and years...

Doze

The fist of night
   relaxed its fingers,

studied quilt texture,
    followed threads circle

a quarter moon as
    the prayer of sleep

ticker-taped the day
    like a child looking

out a car window,
    counting barns on

an evening highway,
    plotless as a bedroom

ceiling before
    first light.

Knock, Knock

In the green morning
I wanted to be a heart.
A heart.
—Lorca

Wake to a sunrise
   in the old farmhouse—

in the orchard,
   apple, pear, peach,

glow spring green
   as creek willows.

You, beside me asleep,
   breath, a hush, a snooze,

how words I learned
   as a child,

consonants, vowels
   whispered,

quiet dawn,
   teach a heart

to pump
   smoothly,

as dewdrops glisten
   tops of grass

before crow calls
knock

a waking day's door
to open.

A Deepening

Clear sky, mockingbird song,
    loop to loop of crows sailing

the breeze. Graveyard clean
    and flowered, porch neighbors

with coffee. Tennessee ridge
    morning above hollows still

edged with night. The soul
    knows this mix is home. Horses

jostle in the Choate's pasture.
    Stillness and slight maple flurry

bring a solitude cicada chirr
    magnifies… not

depression, but a deepening
    with questions: in a warring

country with starving children,
    in trailer down the road littered

with broken toys and stained
    pillows, will young ones know

a grandmother's kitchen with
    jam and biscuits, her strong

hands scrubbing Saturday's dirt
    from their knees?

Certain Words

Cringe, cower, shrink,
  recoil, flinch, blench…

Dramatic words a child
  learns, preparation

for cardinal hitting
  the window, spider

under a pillow, night's
  mirror when leaves

blow against a dark porch.
  Heart in the throat words,

soul's secret closet, every
  life's abandoned home.

Presence recalls absence,
  recoil, a serpent after

it strikes. Cower a child
  at Walmart slapped

by her mother, how
  a girl on a bad date

marries the car door.
  Each life will practice

these words waiting
  for a phone to ring.

Post Contemporary Lorca

My unborn children track me down...
—Lorca

Tonight they are restless.
The youngest can't sleep,
wants to play in the sandbox,
builds a pauper's cemetery
and buries me in an unmarked
grave.

The middle child, who loses
at cards, draws a straight flush
and wins all of my erotic dreams.

The oldest and only daughter
is above all this... her lips blue,
swinging from a noose she made
from my necktie.

Then the ocean collapses,
or the ship sinks, or the bed
mattress threads the eye
of a needle.

Enough, I yell. I promise to
never sleep again. Yea, they
say in unison, like you promised
a pet goat, like you promised us
a mother.

Always

> *Always, these gigantic inconceivables.*
> —C. K. Williams

How they plant themselves
in fear's closet, unexpectedly
expected, even half-desired,
knowing along with life, you
will lose the things you worship:

goldfinch and chickadee,
deer herd and fox kits,
April green and October blue,
heron flight and creek sparkle—
your soft hair-tangle when I wake

at night so all alone. And isn't
this why love and fear of love
always look over our shoulders
to see what isn't coming
and what is.   Outside the pulse's
carnival ride and the price we
pay for a seat, one can choose
to argue with the world or to be
amazed at small hours.
          Cool breeze surprises
a June morning. Even chickadees
choose to share instead of squabble.
A candle shines in a human heart,
however short the wick.

Upon Waking

On a hill where Queen Anne's Lace lay storm-tangled,
a squadron of crows cawed as if a crime had gone unseen.

A half-hearted wish to whistle twisted my lips into a frown.
Somewhere in my past the need to be understood showed up

like a father's ghost, a ghost, whose predawn footsteps
still echoed with his early morning chores. I remembered

our preacher quoting a Bible verse over the phone
the night I called for solace. I was just a boy having

my first experience with death's failure of words.
During another sleepless night, the jury was out,

and the judge fell asleep in his ink. Soon, rain.
I went outside to feel the cold drops hit my face.

St. Simons Morning I

Gandolf beards of Spanish moss
drape live oaks that shade village streets.

I steer my bike in zags to avoid hitting
swifts and lined skinks hunting the walk

for insects. Late June humidity molds
the skin, darkens my shirt with wet—

neck, back, armpits—Atlantic breeze
blocked until I turn on Ocean Blvd.

Palmetto scrubs grow in patches. All
this life formed long before humans

shaped Earth's future toward disaster.
I let this thought rise and disappear

like rainbow bubbles children blow
in the park as the sound of waves

rush the shore, wind flapping wings
of grackles and gulls dancing salty air.

Ancient Jains said *the way to liberation
and bliss is to live a life of harmlessness.*

Perhaps, in the beginning, first humans
learned the words *to be,* the future humans,

   to breathe.

Evening Song

> *Put your mouthful of words away*
> *and come with me to watch...*
> —Anne Sexton

A bright mauve has stolen the horizon,
   brilliant thievery will not last long.
      Night's dark angel will open her book,
         slowly turn the pages as the whippoorwill

sings her song, then hunts the sky with bats.
   Come away from the table where day's
      habits crowd *to dos* to hide the marvel
         of grained maple patinaed with life.

Earth sails the Milky Way. Her little sun
   turns our world toward darkness, but
      gives us its moonlight. Wind in leaves
         stutters pink and navy before the rain crow

tocks her hollow pipe, and the heart's
   small details come to haunt our house,
      try to make it once again a home. *Put*
         your words away and come with me

      to listen.

II

WHAT THE SOUL ATE

What Lasts

> *What lasted is what the soul ate.*
> *The way a child knows the world by putting it*
> *part by part into his mouth...*
> —Jack Gilbert

I

Sixty years ago Uncle Clark threw his cigarette
on the ground before entering our house. At six,
I picked the butt up, put it between my lips like
my mother. How wonderful the taste, the smoke
drifting from my mouth, before the coughing
and having to swallow the spit in the back
of my throat. Campfires of childhood—
the night my brother taught me how to call
barred owls, the last gurgled hoot must curl
up the throat like a bed spring. Bucky's shepherd
puppy raised by his tomcat. An eighty pound
dog, stalked on its knees around a fence to catch
a rabbit. An inseparable pair, canine worshipped
her feline father. Our first little farm house
at Crocker Springs—learning to prune the orchard,
ruthless cutting to open each tree to light. A Key West
night after Ashbery's workshop—a day of poetry,
Mahi, wine and a DJ playing The Drifters for our
last dance. We floated in each other's arms as the sun
wobbled into the sea. Our walks outside of Oxford
along the Thames to the Church at Binsey where
an old woman mowed the graveyard with a push
mower. The sign telling the dogs not to soil the path:
you marveled that Brits taught their dogs to read.

II

Each life has its darkness—
late night calls like night birds
are mostly predatory. Death is
only convenient after long suffering.
It's the price we pay, part of our birthright.
You pass grief around the table
like burnt toast you got as a child,
learn to scrape the dark off
with a spoon and eat it with jelly.

III

Moments stay with us
(*what the soul ate*)—a chuck-will-widow's
song in early spring, our grandniece
feeding an apple to Sonny, the workhorse,
laughing Hispanic children throwing
breadcrumbs to geese. The heart pumps
blood 2.5 billon times in a normal life.
The soul is a-nose-an-eye-an-ear-
a-finger's-touch-a-tongue… how easy
to dismiss *it* as *it* comes—*it,* an impersonal
pronoun—the now—just after—blessed memory—
your hair against your cheek when I awake,
a cracked window breeze, (maybe a ghost
in the attic), or just sounds an old house makes.

Stardust

They were us—two people
two cats—finches at the kitchen window—
screech owl in the night orchard

They touched often—one asleep—one awake
wondering how the earth rushed around a star
while they huddled together

in an antique bed bought at a roadside stand
in Leech, Tennessee—a little hole in the wall
where healers in another century

gathered leeches to bleed the sick—how
if any of this made sense—he didn't get it—
then more sleep—then coffee

Fall maples bloomed red—the earth continued
to bring night in a bowl of stars—they were us
at the window—each holding a spoon

Last Visit

Shadow of the remembered place—
    dogtrot fallen in between bedrooms and kitchen,

no hens bobbing the yard for scraps,
    bream pond, willow choked.

The only well-kept property, the graveyard.
    Crosses poke a sky too big to fathom,

ruled by crows and a circle of vultures.
    Just a two-finger-wave-road

between nowhere and Cub Creek,
    the old school yard fenced in for hogs.

Corn in the bottoms, soy on the hills,
    and factory shifts at the nearest

big town. He doesn't know why
    he brought the old photo album,

family Bible, and his grandfather's
    pocketknife, still blood-sharp.

The Hollow Step

The hollow step up the cabin porch gave a plunk.
Creak of knotty pine led to an open door like scripture.
GrandSally's face, kitchen stove red, her stern smile sunk
Wrinkle lines into her neck. Her aproned self, a gesture

To sit at the oak table for steaming eggs and ham.
Her eyes held stories you prepared yourself to hear:
Come this away, Sadie, howled a panther. Sound
Of grieving barge at night on the Tennessee River,

As it chugged by Lady's Bluff, her scattered bones
Imaged on the rocky shore. Mother of pearl sheened
From mussel shells, an eerie ghost, as the moon shone
Rivulets of current streaming north. Morning dreams

Wake me to Sally's keening voice. Dead these years—
The hollow step, a door that led to scripture.

Arabella

Heirloom she's called,
porcelain smooth doll,

owned by some mother's
mother's mother. From England

it's rumored. An ear bitten
off by an angry sister. Nose

chipped, eyebrows blurred.
She sits in a special chair,

eyes in a constant seizure.
The cat doesn't notice unless

a moth alights on her hair.
Grandnieces change her diapers,

certainly fitting at her age.
I question her value until

I think of what she's seen—
strange fruit hanging from trees,

nightmare trenches WWI,
soup kitchen lines as far

as the eye can reach, beaches,
dead soldier strewn, WWII.

Has anything changed,
I whisper to her. Mum,

she sits proper as can be,
left leg missing a foot,

right leg cropped at the knee.

Church of Childhood

As a child, each morning was a letter
   I could open, a closet with a t-shirt,
     a drawer with darned socks,
       a cold-nosed dog named
         Josephus racing cars.

Sky, a church, earth an altar,
   and I wrote every sermon
     after communion with oatmeal.
       In a maple sheltered yard,
         the dog bowed his head

and licked himself. The garden hose
   sprayed holy water. My sister and I
     christened each other, my underpants
       soggy, my railroad cap befuddled.
         We climbed the magnolia

to sing *I'll Fly Away*,
   loaded cap pistols to play
     Onward Christian Soldiers.
       After Sunday school,
         we choked a coke with peanuts,

the holiest of Sabbath Rituals.
   During communion and preaching,
     we sat like statues
       on the family pew
         and tried not to laugh

when Aunt Mattie's stomach growled.
   We swallowed the flesh,
      wiped the blood of Jesus
         on our shirtsleeves,
            drew pictures in the church bulletin,

and knew
   that
      we
         had
            sinned.

Infant Sun

Light crept past Miss Willie's house,
then quietly sat on our bedroom window.

My bones stretched their joints, covered
my head with a pillow. I dreamt of toast

and peach preserves as maple leaves
clapped in a new day. Crow-crow-crow

on the roof announced its name to the world.
Eyes opened to moon-green of a Luna moth

asleep on the glass, long antennas peeking
in like eyes. Clop, clop of horse and wagon,

and a man sang out his selling song of *cow
manure, aged, stacked and ready, Freddy.*

The Korean War ended and headlines
praised the dead. Two young men on our street

wouldn't wake, as I had, to hometown
harmonies of another morning, and grief

in its black scarf inhabited porches.
Yet, old Mo whistled *The Tennessee Waltz*

next door. Wags, our spaniel, hid in hedge
to bark at the postman. Mother's roses,

red, yellow and orange, too bright for sorrow,
danced a jig with the infant sun.

County Braille

Tree shadows,
    cotton wood, ash, sycamore,
reach like God's fingers
    to read the braille
of a scarred county road—
    psalm of cicada chirr,
swallowtail wings
    and crumpled beer cans.
A string of cars
    circles the cemetery
like a wagon train;
    reminding me
of an argument I dreamed
    with a dead friend.
I awoke feeling absurd,
    like the day I called
my mother for a recipe
    two months after her death:
how many eggs
    for a squash casserole?
Then grief came back,
    smothered me, facing
darkness inside
    with new eyes, like
waking in the morning
    to a night window.
Yet,
    my mother would
laugh at my idiocy—
    tell me *two eggs
and don't forget the cheese;*
    my friend would

slap me on the back.
I'm dead, he'd say,
the argument's over,
you win.

Hilltop Musings

From the green hilltop, freshly mown,
    a limestone shelf pokes tips of ancient
        fossils for the sun to warm. Perhaps
some memory still feels the shallow
    sea that provided home and food
        for creatures to survive. Perhaps not.
Though I sit on one outcrop and finger
    its rough surface, imagine life after
        life after life, find myself out of breath,
fill my lungs with May air, exhale
    and fill again. Breathing, itself a form
        of prayer, an ageless mantra despite
one cloud overhead and the scratchy
    fuss of sapsucker in the sycamore.
        My dead Mother's answer always:
Hope springs eternal. Today, my past
    is a fossil of sorts, *Eternal,* meaningless.
        My dreams, a slideshow of faces, places,
many I don't know, but in the dreams do.
    So this morning from the fossil strewn
        hill, I'll just say *hope springs.* From
a distance, I imagine the sun sparkle
    Snow Creek, as my neighbor sharpens
        his tools in the shed, whistling something
Hank Williams, and I know my 67th year
    on this planet is worth living. One day
        my ashes will be scattered and little
chunks of crowned teeth might be left
    for some paleontologist to speculate.
        My dust will take other shapes in this
ongoing miracle. My empty coffee cup
    seeks my attention. *One more cup of*
        coffee for the road, Mr. Dylan.

Traffic Salvation

You were meant to wake at 5 a.m.
to follow four car lengths
behind the one in front
in freeway traffic.
The man behind will ride
your bumper, shake his fist,
twist his lips to say
your mother is canine
and unmarried.
Think damn you, God
stuck you on this freeway
to be tempted—the billboards,
Chequeeta Tequilla wearing
tight bathing apparel,
the Canadian Silk Goddess
beckoning you to join her
on the bearskin rug.
Your lust will get you plastered
to the back of a stalled
eighteen wheeler. Listen closely,
there is salvation in traffic.
Pray at the wheel. Give thanks
for the station wagon from Indiana,
the Thurston Trucking Company,
McCleans, Lone Star Transport,
pray for all the trucking son's
mothers. The mothers' truckers
will find redemption, will die saved
and not jackknifed to hell
on that final slick. Take heed,
the second coming will arrive
at rush hour. Road construction
will delay traffic for eternity.

Jesus will descend in a Dodge Duster
and hover above the Holy Toll Booth.
He has paid your fee.

Morning Instructions

Drive off Ridge Top, down the curvy rope
of Tinnen Hollow, level on a creek road

open to cedar wind toss. Put your tongue
to the roof of your mouth, say sacred,

not die, go to heaven sacred, but one more
morning song in the reverence of solitude.

Say the word cynical, roll down your window
and spit—watch a small flock of waxwings

eat juniper berries. Listen to them whisper
to each other as they feed—say earth, feel

your tongue click your teeth with the "th."
Say dirt, water, air and sunlight are God.

Whisper creek burble, Bubby, Momma, Papa—
feel your lips nurse the words. Now, follow

the white arms of sycamore as they caress
the sky—a sharp-shinned hawk will be waiting.

Night Creek with Goats

A light rain mists Baker Station Road.
Cat Creek trickles beneath a limestone ridge.

My hands feel soft on steering wheel
as I slow to savor an S curve where

goats amble against the fence.
No headlights but mine…

I stop to visit black glistening noses
and bright eyes, na-na-na-na, one says.

A peace embraces night herd animals,
beautiful goatees hang over the top wire.

I never thought of goats as innocent,
but this evening loves them, makes them

beautiful and wise. I hit the light switch
and embrace their darkness. Maybe I feel

beautiful and wise as well. A light rain
will raise the creek from trickle to run to roll—

the shoals will sing for goats
on an anonymous Tennessee night.

And I should ease to the straightaway
before turning on the lights.

Some days

start open and end in a tunnel.
Memory salvages what it can, vestiges

of morning sun, leaf flutter, church bells,
matins, a golden scatter of finches.

Pink and mauve leave thumbprints
on early evening's hymn and hush.

Another day, billed and spent,
shuts her eyes and ends up home.

Sleep

...Fall gently and keep him in the civil wilderness of sleep...
—Robert Herrick

A friend's death brings back a game
  of hide and seek when we were children,
    backyard lilies and giant oaks.

Wind in leaves—a wave sweeping
  a beach, a distant sail on a tall ship,
    an attic fan in my first home pulling

fresh air through each room.
  A light opening a cloud seam
    in the winter sky where two

snowflakes dance down
  to find the window. Somewhere
    in the heart's dictionary

a word is misspelled,
  a preposition forgets its object,
    an action verb is served with cream.

In the closet's heart valve
  a clot dissolves, an artery
    widens to accept a sister's

idea of faith—belief
  sneezes and the red fringe
    of a universe is born.

Sunrise at the Cemetery

This morning the dead are silent,
like my father's silence. Sometimes

his empty face spoke volumes—
battle artillery blazing, Japanese soldiers

jumping off cliffs on Suicide Island,
Kamikaze planes spinning into crowded ships—

all of this shared by my brother long
after Dad's death. Yet, he was a man

whose tongue kept songs and stories.
Sometimes his silence bore a smile—

his boyhood on the Tennessee River,
freshwater pearls and arrowheads,

how moving water found a quiet place
that opened him to joy—blue eyes

sparkling enough to make woodland
violets jealous. It's seven o'clock

and a daytime moon floats the sky
like a silver shell. Names on tombstones

blur in my vision. Two crows alight
on a marble cross to greet morning.

Herons fly to wetlands in the Mississippi
bottoms. The landscape whispers my father's

name—wind in trees, rush of shoals, swirl
of deep current, ghost of weathered barns.

My father was a righteous man, he taught
this is right and this wrong. After his death,

my sins still present, fished for and caught
like bluegill, cleaned and cooked,

    flesh divided from the bones.

Seeing

Your face in a night window,
Look beyond its reflection to

Shadows trees make in moonlight.
Among them you might

Find your father smoking,
The cigarette tip glowing

As he draws in smoke,
His face pensive, less

Strained than the year
Before his death.

There, right there, he pointed
To a moving eddy behind a rock

Where he knew you'd catch a trout.
Here, right here, he'd hold his glove,

Signaling a strike. And *yonder,*
Always *yonder,* when he directed

Your eyes to a place too far to see.
When his hands were busy,

He pointed with his chin,
Or caught your eyes with

His and gazed where
Yours should follow.

Verbs

Two miles into my walk
the word *be* appears on my tongue,
a short verb that seeds dream,
that creation, in its understandable
domain, seems to know well,
to be, not to be and to be again,
the somethingness of existence.
Crow in sumac watches with keen eyes.
Oak leaf on the grass with sharp
points says pin oak, its name—
how the world worded itself
into existence is human, is bird,
is tree—each with its own sense
of being. Fungus and mold
make a home for oak roots,
say thank you for sugar in return.
And I, in my own impatience,
let pass what is life in each moment.
I'll try to make this a *Be* walk
until my mind flashes back
to England, Vermont, Idaho,
Virginia, or even a small mountain
creek named Laurel that flows
into the North River in Tennessee,
once a native trout stream until
road construction opened
a bauxite deposit that killed it;
what we remember once was.
I notice the orange-spotted
head of a tortoise beneath
yellow coreopsis—
both flowers of sorts—
the morning itself
a blossom. Be and
Was and Will Be.

My Mother

On the little street of my birth,
my mother traced children's
handprints pressed in dirt,
named them Barbara, Linda Jo
or Donny.
She spied a feather,
named it mockingbird,
waxwing or finch,
folded it in a tissue
and placed it in her pocket.
The sky often found
her staring at trees
as if their murmur in wind
was other than leaves,
and the way she lingered
to listen followed
a sorrow of air.
She smoothed tables,
collars, sleeves, with hands
caressing, blessing the clothes
we wore, surfaces we shared
at breakfast.
As long as she lived, there
were candlesticks, morning
windows, and late night
creaks on the stairs.
Feathers began to appear
in hats, in windows
open to breeze, in gardens
beside her favorite roses.
Doctors cracked her chest,
spread her ribs, cleared
her heart.

She lived two years,
and when she died,
a sorrow of air,
murmur of trees,
of birds.

House

> *What we speak becomes the house we live in.*
> —Hafez

Fall backwards, the paper reads.
So we set the clock from twelve
to eleven, feel a night breeze
drift from porch, and listen
to the mockingbird sing its
territorial rendition of finch,
titmouse, crow, wren, towhee.
How paying attention
makes the world specific
and the nouns that name it.
The boy inside the man
remembers being taught
birdsongs and the mythos
of plant names—bloodroot,
Dutchman's britches, aster.
Yahweh commanded Adam
to name, so the garden became
the house they lived in. And
even after The Fall, nothing
could stop the naming, as
humans became little gods,
fearful of death. HAFEZ, how
we speak the words sets a tone,
decorates the house, makes it
a home. Patina of kitchen table
where our family held court,
Grandmother's dishes we ate
from on Sundays, Grandfather's
rocker reserved for Father, each
family's oral book of rules.

The man the boy became knows
that what we speak can also make an
empty house with broken windows.

Ness

*(English suffix attached to adjectives and participles,
forming abstractions denoting quality and state)*

Aloneness caresses
    the tops of trees,

looks over stone
    cliffs into valleys,

perches on a birch
    branch,

kingfisher
    surveying a stream.

Loneliness is
    a closed window,

an unmade bed,
    a place in the head

that slumps
    shoulders,

fingers touching
    one's face.

Aloneness is a mow
    hole stacked with hay,

a barn door opened
    by wind,

the sound of rain on
    forest loam,

a field where chicory
    roams blue in a breeze.

Redecorate

To redecorate my yard
    I give you wren call,

upside down balance
    of nuthatch, whirly-gig

maple seed coptering
    away from its mother

to sprout among basil.
    Rainbow dew spider web,

I fold into primary colors
    and tuck away for August.

Buzzard shadow, crow caw
    from church steeple, purple

bib of grackle in sun
    brightens the memory

of my father's death,
    how his dog wept until

it found its own darkness.
    The first memory—wet

underwear while dancing
    around the sprinkler

with neighborhood kids,
    I save as a helping of

innocence to brighten
my shadow self,

stuffed with years
of turning away.

Goodnight Shadows

—for C and B

Overheard outside a boy's bedroom:
*Goodnight shadows, goodnight shadows, how
long will I tell shadows goodnight?*

Brian, our shadows live with us as
    long as we live, sometimes leaping

forward, sometimes trailing behind,
    other times standing even, depending

on the sun's direction to our spinning.
    Sometimes ours is overshadowed

by maple, house, or father.
    Yet who would not want this

absence of light exacting our shape
    as we follow our paths.

But if you're talking to shadows that creep
    your bed at night, think of them

as the ones you create when you miss
    your own—as artful as

herons drifting a lake,
    woeful as buzzards circling

county roads or oak limbs
    surveying the earth.

Think of your shadow as
    a life's study in the sun.

Praise for *The Headless Angel*

[A] scent / …softens my old man's shoulders …. Nature and memory fill Brown's latest collection with joy and sorrow. *The Headless Angel* celebrates our interconnectedness with nature and how much we benefit creatively and spiritually by what she offers. Packed with wisdom and candor, these meditative poems explore the choices we make; like a child first learning the wonders of this world, we *can choose / to argue with the world or to be / amazed at small hours*. Brown's anchor is family: that sacred place where shadows of secrets kept or stories told around the table continue to haunt our dreams. The ghosts of those closest to us crowd the garden where the headless angel keeps watch. Sensuous language revels in both light and darkness, *knowing along with life, you / will lose the things you worship*. In the current climate of clamor and distrust, the echo of Brown's finely crafted words enrich our lives, enfold us with words of comfort. And we will return to them again and again.

—KB Ballentine

Whether the humor of "Traffic Salvation," with its word play and on-spot descriptions of the modern world's least-favorite pastime, or the prayers imbedded in "On a Cloudy August Day," "Waiting, September Morning," "Today's News," and many others, the poems in Bill Brown's latest collection, *The Headless Angel*, are more than reward for a few hours spent in their company. The natural world of "crows jostling each other in flight," "a white oak cathedral filled with starlings," and "red maple buds whispering birth" blend with the joys of home—"a maple table patinaed with living," "an antique bed bought at a roadside stand"—to create poems that place the reader in the immediacy of a well-considered and well-loved life.

—Connie Jordan Green

Bill Brown is the author of twelve poetry collections and a writing textbook, *Important Words*, on which he collaborated with Malcolm Glass. In 1999 Brown wrote and co-produced the Instructional Television Series, *Student Centered Learning,* for Nashville Public Television. Brown directed the writing program at Hume-Fogg Academic High School in Nashville for 19 years. His philosophy that those who write live more examined lives fostered a love of words in generations of students. He retired from Hume-Fogg in May 2003 and accepted a part-time lecturer's position at Peabody College of Vanderbilt University. In 1995 the National Foundation for Advancement in the Arts named him Distinguished Teacher in the Arts. He has been a Scholar in Poetry at the Bread Loaf Writers Conference, a Fellow at the Virginia Center for the Creative Arts, and a two-time recipient of Individual Artist Fellowships in poetry from the Tennessee Arts Commission. In 2011 the Tennessee Writers Alliance awarded Brown Writer of the Year. He continues to do consultant work and lead writing workshops. He and his wife Suzanne live in the hills of Robertson County with a tribe of cats.

www.ingramcontent.com/pod-product-compliance
Lightning Source LLC
Chambersburg PA
CBHW022118090426
42743CB00008B/911